Old is Not a Four-Letter Word

A Midlife Guide

ANN E. GERIKE, PHD

ILLUSTRATIONS BY PETER KOHLSAAT

PAPIER-MACHE PRESS

WATSONVILLE, CA

01 00 99 98 97   5 4 3 2 1

ISBN: 1-57601-002-3 Softcover

Cover and interior illustrations © 1997 by Peter Kohlsaat
Design and composition by Elysium
Copyediting by Lynn Leslie
Proofreading by Shirley Coe
Author photograph by Hilary N. Bullock
Manufactured by Malloy Lithographing, Inc.

Library of Congress Cataloging-in-Publication Data
Gerike, Ann E., 1933–
     Old is not a four-letter word / Ann E. Gerike; illustrations by Peter Kohlsaat.
          p.   cm.
     Includes bibliographical references.
     ISBN 1-57601-002-3 (alk. paper))
     1. Middle aged persons—United States—Psychology. 2. Middle aged persons—United States—
Attitudes. 3. Aging—United States—Psychological aspects. 4. Midlife crisis—United States. I. Title.
HQ1059.5.U5G47   1997
305.244—dc21   97-494
                                                                              CIP

⊕ This book is printed on acid-free, recycled paper containing a minimum of 85 percent total recycled fiber with 15 percent postconsumer de-inked fiber.

To

Barbara Kohlsaat
(1915–1995)

and

Grace Warfield
(1909–1990)

Contents

Special thanks

from Ann to Susan Perry, in whose course the book was spawned and who supported, advised, and encouraged throughout; to Michael Sigrin, who first suggested she "lighten up" and use cartoons; and to the members of her writing group, Barbara Gill and Rita Johnson, whose skills and enthusiasm improved and enlivened the text. She acknowledges all the activists whose work preceded hers, and is grateful to her large extended family and many friends for their support and encouragement—especially David, Peggy, Cathy, Sam, Eunice, Esther, and the light of her life, Jeremiah.

Peter and Ann thank each other, and all the people who have aged before them.

Old

is Not a

Four-Letter

Word

A Midlife Guide

Introduction

In the Sands of Denial

We're all growing older.
And if we're lucky,
we'll *keep* growing older
for a long time.

But if you're like most
people, you don't want to
think about it. You've got
your head firmly planted
in the sands of denial.

You don't want to think about it
because you're constantly being told that growing older means

losing your looks,

losing your memory,

losing your mind,

losing your physical abilities,

losing your sex appeal

and your power to perform.

Not so!!

6

Dump those ideas!

Get with it!

Move into the twenty-first century!

Now that the people who study aging
are growing older, they're finding
that it's not so bad after all.

They're finding that people their age
and even much older can be

$$T = E \left(M \sqrt[3]{3} \frac{v}{q} k \right.$$

intelligent,

attractive,

witty and interesting,

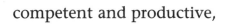

competent and productive,

and even (gasp!)

s e x u a l !

They're also finding that many
of the problems they blamed on aging
are not caused by aging at all,
but by habits that can be changed.

What growing older does mean is

change.

You've been changing ever since you were born,
so you know how to do it.

Resisting change is what causes problems!

Growing older has some real advantages,
but you don't hear much about them
in our youth-obsessed society.

Accepting all the garbage you hear about aging
can make you depressed and anxious.
It can turn you against yourself.
It can keep you from enjoying the rest of your life.

So read on!

What have you got to lose?
A few bucks, and a little time.

And what do you have to gain?
A change in attitude that can change your life.

Chapter One

You Look Great for Your Age

The Myth of Loss of Looks

Mom?

You Look Great for Your Age

The Myth of Loss of Looks

If you're like a lot of boomers, you don't really *look* at yourself in the mirror all that often.

You may focus on certain areas while you're applying make-up, or shaving, or combing your hair. You may sneak a broader peek when the light's bad, or you don't have your glasses on, or you're ten feet from the mirror.

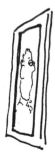

The face you see, when you do happen to catch a glimpse of it, may look disconcertingly like your father's or your mother's.

If you believe in the Myth of Loss of Looks, you probably don't like what you see.

This myth tells you that you become less attractive the older you get (especially if you're female) and implies that, if you live to be old, you'll be ugly.

If anyone has ever paid you the ultimate noncompliment, "You're not bad-looking for someone your age," you've been a victim of this myth.

Any society that really believes the old are ugly has a major visual impairment.

A smooth surface is not superior to a textured one,
just different.

Imagine how boring the world would be if everyone looked alike.

Now, having established that you are a sane person
in a crazy world—

take a good long look in the mirror.

What do you see?

A face and body that's been with you quite a while, and has carried you through some tough times.

If you have a lifelong friend who's been with you through thick and thin, you're probably very fond of him (or her). You're probably loving, kind, and forgiving, not expecting him (or her) to be perfect.

So why treat yourself like an enemy—criticizing, ridiculing, or scolding yourself for not being what you used to be?

You can become
your own best friend.

Instead of thinking about what you've lost, consider what you've gained.

Your face is much more interesting than it used to be. The older you get, the more distinctive it becomes. Lines add variety to an otherwise bland surface.

You are, in fact, creating your own face, by your habitual thoughts and expressions.

If you've been coloring your hair, think about letting it be itself. Hair often greys in unusual patterns. And as it changes color, along with your skin tone, you may find yourself able to wear colors that had not suited you before.

If you're a woman, think of your breasts as beginning to relax, after a lifetime of straining to be the perfect perky ideal (which, for most of us, they never achieved anyway).

If you're a balding man, think of your scalp as emerging boldly from its unnecessary hair disguise.

And if you've put on a little weight—or a lot (especially around the middle, hence the term "middle" age)—think of yourself as having cuddlier body lines.

If you stop criticizing your face and body, and begin to treat yourself well, you'll probably find yourself looking—and feeling—better.

And the more you genuinely love yourself, body and soul, the more other people are likely to do so as well.

Few things are more attractive than a person, of any age, who feels good about herself (or himself), and is enjoying life.

Chapter Two

I'd Like You to Meet Whatsisname

The Myth of Memory Loss

I'd Like You to Meet Whatsisname

The Myth of Memory Loss

You've been forgetting all your life, but you never paid much attention to it before.

Now, when you can't remember a name, or you find your-self at the top of the stairs and wonder

why you went up there, you begin to fear that it's the Beginning of the End.

Many people believe that losing memory is a normal part of growing older. It isn't.

The vast majority of people over sixty-five have no major memory problems. Even after the age of ninety, approximately 70 percent of people function without serious difficulties.

But there is *change*. What happens, at least for most people, is that memory slows down. Your brain's more sophisticated than it used to be, but it takes a little longer to sort out details.

As with your computer, you may sometimes have to wait a while before the information you want pops onto your screen. There's a lot more in your hard drive now than there was when you were twenty.

And because memory is a complex process, other problems may affect it.

To remember something, you first have to see, hear, smell, taste, or touch it; pay attention to it; concentrate on it; rehearse it; and move it from short-term to long-term storage.

A failure anywhere along the line can cause problems.

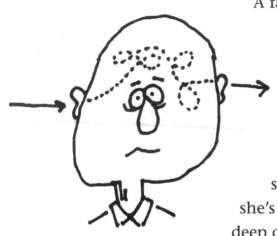

If you've been to one too many rock concerts, you literally may not hear what's being said, or may mis hear it. (If she says, "Phone me at six," and you hear, "Joan says she's sick," you'll probably be in deep doo-doo.)

You're less likely to remember what the trainer wrote on the flip chart if you couldn't quite see it.

And if your significant other is talking to you about his (or her) plans for Saturday, and most of your attention is occupied by the call you should have made before you left the office, you'll forget to press "Save." And what he (or she) said won't be in your memory.

(Obviously, this chapter provides you with a whole new set of excuses for your next heated disagreement!)

If your system is overloaded—if you're depressed, anxious, or feeling a lot of stress in general—you're more likely to forget things. Worrying about your memory can make it even worse.

Some antidepressants and blood pressure medications can cause memory problems, as can some illnesses.

And alcohol and drug abuse can produce major memory glitches. If you have serious concerns about your memory, check with your doctor.

You can learn strategies to improve your memory, and practice them. For example, a good way to remember someone's name is to repeat it after you've been introduced: "Merrily Werollalong, nice to meet you."

See the Reading List at the back of this book for more ways to improve your memory. Just as with your body, stretching your memory keeps it in shape. In fact, getting more physical exercise may also help your memory by getting more blood into your brain.

Or you can do what I do—buy a bunch of self-stick notepads and write notes to yourself, listing whatever you want to take to work and posting it in front of the door, so that you'll fall over it on your way out in the morning! (This works best if you're the first—or only— one out the door.)

As people move beyond middle age, they may experience more changes. Instead of being able to do five things at once, they may be able to manage only one or two. They may be more likely to forget things if you interrupt them. But they haven't *lost* their memories, just temporarily misplaced them. And many old people say they don't *want* to remember everything.

There are, of course, real illnesses and diseases that cause memory loss, especially strokes and Alzheimer's disease. They're very distressing, but far from inevitable.

One last suggestion: Start keeping track of how often younger people forget things. Your memory may not be as bad as you think it is.

Chapter Three

How Is It Possible to Know Less When You've Learned More?

The Myth of Inevitable Mental Decline

Vrrrrrrooooooom!

How Is It Possible to Know Less When You've Learned More?

The Myth of Inevitable Mental Decline

Do you believe that, as you get older, you'll lose not only your memory but all your other mental abilities as well?

If you do, you're a victim of MIMD—the Myth of Inevitable Mental Decline.

The sad result of such a belief is that, as you get older, you won't try anything new because you don't believe you can learn, grow, and change.

So you end up being bored, boring, and depressed.

Big mistake!

By being mentally active, you can actually enrich your brain. (Or at least rats did, so you probably can too.)

When old rats were put into a kind of McDonald's playground and then "sacrificed" (on the altar of science, no doubt), their little brains were found to have sprouted some new connectors (dendrites) on their nerve cells (neurons)—unlike the brains of old rats who just sat around in their cages all day without even a TV to watch.

And it's those connections between cells that make for a livelier brain.

Again, *change* is the password.

Crystallized intelligence, the sum total of everything you've learned, increases as you grow older, especially if you're mentally active. It includes the number of words you know; the general information you've picked up from reading, watching TV, and talking with people; and how well you understand that information.

Learning may in some ways become easier, because you know a little bit about a lot of things and have more hooks on which to hang new information.

On the other hand, *fluid intelligence,* your ability to process information rapidly, tends to decrease. If the clock's ticking away while the melody plays and the emcee is reminding you that time is passing, you're less likely to shine.

Recently, people in their eighties who volunteered to have their thinking tested did as well as people in their thirties and forties, when they weren't being pressed for time. (They were probably a lively minded bunch who thought they'd do well—and did.)

Those who did begin to show mental decline were generally less active and involved in life, less flexible in their thinking, less healthy, and (not surprisingly) less satisfied with their lives. And even they didn't begin much of a downhill slide until their mid-sixties.

One of the cardinal rules of aging is that, the longer people live, the more different they become from each other.

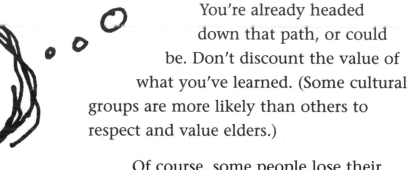

I have lived... therefore I am.

Some people become wise, learning from their successes and failures, from surviving hard times, from living.

You're already headed down that path, or could be. Don't discount the value of what you've learned. (Some cultural groups are more likely than others to respect and value elders.)

Of course, some people lose their mental abilities because of disease or illness or accidents. Sometimes, though not always, these occur at older ages, and through no failure or fault of your own. But you can increase your likelihood of being a mentally alert older person by being a mentally alert younger one.

Your brain, like your car, won't do well if it just sits in the garage all day.

Take it out for a spin!

Vrrrrrooooom!

Learn something new. If your job is boring, find something else in life that's interesting. Sprout some dendrites on those neurons!

It's never too soon to start.

Chapter Four

The Midlife Crossover: It Can Both Lift and Separate

The Midlife Crossover: It Can Both Lift and Separate

Women! Are you finding yourself more assertive, more competent, more willing to speak your mind as you get older? Do you find yourself itching to get on with what you want to do—for yourself, not for other people?

Men! Are you becoming more tenderhearted, finding yourself more "in touch with your feelings"? Are you tired of being competitive? Would like to relax and enjoy life more with your friends and/or your family?

If so, welcome to the great Midlife Crossover.

David Gutmann, a psychologist from Northwestern University, has written a whole book about this subject. He's found it happening all over the world, in many different cultures.

Carl Jung, a Swiss psychologist, wrote about it way back in 1933.

But a lot of people still haven't heard about it, so they're surprised when it starts to happen.

Obviously, we are again talking about our old friend,

change!

If you're a man who's tried to do the male thing—be a rock at all times and battle it out in a tough world—you may think there's something wrong with you when you begin to wonder: Is this necessary, or even possible?

You may get depressed, or even feel trapped and have panic attacks, if you believe that women—especially a spouse or significant other—expect you to be rock solid.

But if you let the changes happen, you may find yourself enjoying life more than ever before, and have better relationships with friends and family.

If you're a woman, you may get grumpy or depressed as this Crossover time approaches. You feel all this energy rising up inside you, and you aren't sure what might happen if you let it all come out. Maybe a husband or significant other will feel threatened, and leave. And what will you *do* with all that energy?

Holding it down is hard work; no wonder you're grumpy!

Women usually find that, when they let nature take its course, they emerge as their true and complete selves, and say they feel better than ever before in their lives.

Obviously, with such changes taking place, male/female relationships can become a little wacky (though the common belief that divorce rates are highest in midlife is not true). Women and men need to accept the changes not only in themselves, but in their partners.

If you're a woman, you may become frightened when it seems to you that your "Rock of Gibraltar" is crumbling, regardless of how much you've bemoaned his being out of touch with his feelings. If he wants to give up a well-paying job he hates for a riskier venture he's yearned for all his life, that's going to be scary for you, regardless of whether you're in the work force or not, especially if you have children.

47

If you're a man, you may be puzzled by the anger or depression that often precede these changes in a woman. And then you may feel abandoned when a woman who previously took care of you, the house, and the family (even if you did some of it and she worked outside the home) begins to pay more attention to herself and what she wants. Her new focus, determination, and independence may frighten you.

Make your own meatloaf.

However, when both women and men know that these changes are normal and expectable, they may be able to make this Midlife Crossover without knocking each other off the bridge in the process. Actually, the changes balance each other out very nicely, and make it possible for each person to be a more complete human being.

Chapter Five

For Women and Those Who Love Them

The Myth of Menopausal Madness

For Women and Those Who Love Them

The Myth of Menopausal Madness

For a while, it seemed that the Myth of Menopausal Madness was about to be buried. However, vampire-like, it has risen again, nourished by the specter of menopause as an "Estrogen Deficiency Disorder," rather than a normal life change which has been successfully negotiated by millions of middle-aged and old women.

Despite recent descriptions of menopause that make it sound like an excruciating and far-from-silent passage (made bearable only by a flick of the magic estrogen wand), for the majority of women, menopause is no big deal.

Most older women, looking back, see it as a blip on the screen of their lives. Unless it was surgical menopause, it was so stretched out that they just lived their way through it without a lot of fuss.

Meno-hardly-any-pause-at-all

On the other hand, some women do have real problems, which deserve treatment. Whether you use estrogen therapies or other remedies for severe hot flashes, night sweats, vaginal dryness, or other problems is up to you and your doctor.

Increasingly, physicians are recommending HRT (Hormone Replacement Therapy) for a variety of reasons, including offsetting osteoporosis and heart disease, but there is still a lot of controversy about its long-term use.

The basic problem, of course, is that there was no good research on women until recently, so we'll have the answers we need about twenty years from now—a little late for most of us. (See the back of this book for resources to help you make informed decisions about your choices now.)

Though osteoporosis is a real concern for some women, it's not a problem for everyone. We heavier women have an edge here, in part because some estrogen is produced by fat cells, and in part because we do weight-bearing exercise (which helps produce strong bones) every time we move!

Menopause does not cause depression, though you may get depressed at this time of your life, as well as at any other time. Depression is treatable with psychotherapy or counseling, and/or medications. (See "A Therapist's Afterword.")

Sometimes women get depressed at this age because they believe the Myth of Loss of Looks. If you're trying too hard to look younger than you are, you'll probably end up looking strained and exhausted. Relax!

And if you're paired with a younger man—an increasingly common combination—don't ask him why he's with someone your age. Instead, compliment him on his good judgment and good fortune.

Your sexual interest may increase (especially knowing you won't get pregnant). Or it may decrease, or stay the same. There will be some changes in your sexual apparatus, which will probably require creams and lubricants to make you more comfortable. But you can continue to have orgasms into old age, if you want to, either with a partner or alone.

For years, I have referred to hot flashes as "power surges," because so many women come into their personal power at this stage of life, via the good old Midlife Crossover.

Women who live in societies that value older women have fewer problems at menopause. So if you begin to like yourself more—and to challenge all the put-downs of women's aging in this society—you may be less likely to experience menopause as a problem and more likely to see it as a "change whose time has come."

Chapter Six

For Men and Those Who Love Them

Temporary Power Outage, or Why Don't You Come When I Call You?

For Men and Those Who Love Them

Temporary Power Outage, or Why Don't You Come When I Call You?

It's estimated that 40 to 70 percent of men over forty have at least an occasional episode of "male erectile dysfunction," commonly labeled impotence—an unfortunate word that, like the experience, can leave you feeling powerless.

I have renamed these episodes TPOs—Temporary Power Outages, a much more hopeful term.

You've probably been hit with a TPO occasionally. But if it keeps happening, don't try to ignore it and think it will go away by itself. You and your partner will probably have a very long wait, and your relationship will suffer.

There are reasons for TPOs, and most of them have nothing to do with what's going on in your head.

About 85 percent of persistent TPOs have a physical cause.

More than two hundred prescription drugs, including some anti-depressants, can contribute to the problem, as can some over-the-counter medications. Diabetes is a frequent culprit.

And if you're a heavy cigarette smoker, and/or a heavy user of alcohol and drugs, you'll probably have more and more TPOs.

When in doubt, check it out. Read labels and prescription drug information; talk to your doctor if you're having problems. Often a prescription can be changed.

Depression is another source of TPOs, or lack of interest in sex, and almost everything else for that matter. It's treatable with therapy or counseling and/or antidepressants. (Just be sure not to get one that causes TPOs!)

It's possible that the old Midlife Crossover may even be the source of an occasional TPO. If you're accustomed to having sex primarily as a physical act, and suddenly find that you're having tender thoughts and feelings about your partner, that may throw you temporarily. But in the long run, it's likely to improve your sex life.

Whatever you do, don't blame a TPO on your partner's presumed lack of attractiveness unless you really want to destroy the relationship.

One of the normal changes that takes place with age is, as with memory, a slowing down: it takes longer for a man to get a full erection. He may think it's a TPO, but given time and stimulation, he'll be back to his old self. If, however, he thinks it's a reflection on his manhood, or his feelings about his partner, they both may be heading down the road to major problems.

Women tend to take TPOs less seriously than men do. They do not fully appreciate the control issues involved, never having had an appendage with a mind of its own (so to speak).

If you have a willing and understanding partner, there are strategies that you can try together when TPOs become a problem. There are also medical and other treatments.

In any event, even persistent TPOs don't have to mean the end of your sex life. Sex is, after all, more than "the act."

Be creative!

Chapter Seven

I Have a Brother and Sister, So My Parents Must Have Done It Three Times

Changing Attitudes toward Sexuality

I Have a Brother and Sister, So My Parents Must Have Done It Three Times

Changing Attitudes toward Sexuality

As your basic sexual equipment gradually changes at midlife, you may also find changes taking place in your attitudes toward sexuality.

When you were a kid and found out how babies were produced, you probably thought no one would *want* to do something so gross any more often than necessary.

Maybe you're still uncomfortable with the thought of your parents having sex (whether or not they're still married to each other). So now that you're parent-aged, you don't have sex for fun either, right?

Well, sometimes you do and sometimes you don't. A lot of you, married or single, partnered or unpartnered, may have found yourselves having sex with surprising irregularity.

And even more surprisingly, in our sexually obsessed society, you may find that that's OK with you, at least some of the time.

You may be working long hours building a career. You may be running to several jobs to support yourself and your children.

You may be exhausted from caring for a new baby. You may not have a partner at the moment. Or you may just not be all that interested.

A recent survey found that married and cohabiting couples aged thirty to sixty-five "do it" on an average of 3.2 times a month (the .2 occurring no doubt when they're just getting started and one of the kids knocks on the door).

It also produced the startling information that singles have sex less often than marrieds—a statistic which comes as a surprise to very few singles, most of whom don't have someone handy in the bed every night or in the kitchen every morning.

(Interestingly, this study didn't look at the sex lives of people over sixty-five, apparently assuming that a Social Security check takes the place of sex. Wrong. See Robert Butler's *Love and Sex after Sixty.*)

With women's increasing assertiveness and men's new awareness of their feelings, sex as you grow older can be fuller, richer, more meaningful, or more relaxed and more fun—even though (or possibly because?) it's less frequent. You'll probably also find yourself becoming less obsessive about performance and enjoying the other person more—body, mind, and spirit.

Sex begins to fall into place as you gain in years. It's not, after all, like food, air, and water, something that you will die without. And some people never liked it all that much to begin with.

Some who like it, and some who don't, choose celibacy, at least temporarily. If you decide on that, and are not in a relationship, it's your own business and not a sign that there's something wrong with you. In fact, a period of celibacy can be an excellent time to focus on yourself and find out who you are when you're not part of a couple.

As for falling in love, you can do that at any age, and it's still the same irrational, delightful, earthshaking, bell-ringing event.

Chapter Eight

Do You Really *Want* to Climb Mountains When You're Eighty-Four?

The Myth of Inevitable Physical Decay

Help.

Do You Really *Want* to Climb Mountains When You're Eighty-Four?

The Myth of Inevitable Physical Decay

Let's face it. Your body at fifty is not the same as it was at twenty-five. But getting older does *not* mean that you will fall apart. You're not destined to become a collection of rusted-out nonfunctioning parts, sitting miserably on top of the junk heap of life.

You're certainly more likely to have some physical problems as you get older—though many of these are not due to aging itself, but to things you did or didn't do when you were younger (including yesterday).

For example, if you played a lot of contact sports, or had a few skiing accidents, your joints and tendons are probably complaining about now. If you've smoked cigarettes all your life, your heart and lungs will know about it.

Help.

And if your primary exercise is walking to the refrigerator, your body may be calling for help!

As you become fonder of your body, having been with (or in) it longer, now is a good time to begin healthier habits. It's never too late to start. People who begin strength training show improvement at any age, even in their eighties and nineties. But you may not want to wait that long.

Start paying attention to newspaper and magazine stories about the physical achievements of people older than fifty. Many of them were couch potatoes until midlife. They report that they feel better physically now than they did twenty years ago.

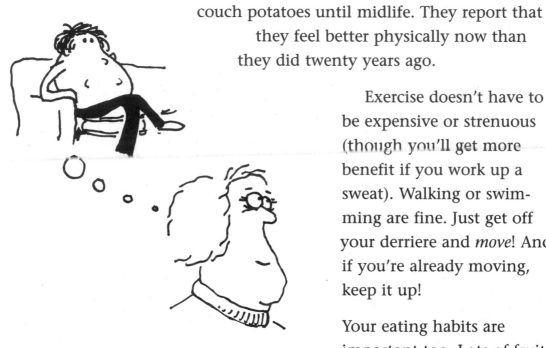

Exercise doesn't have to be expensive or strenuous (though you'll get more benefit if you work up a sweat). Walking or swimming are fine. Just get off your derriere and *move*! And if you're already moving, keep it up!

Your eating habits are important too. Lots of fruits and vegetables, not much meat and fat, plenty of complex carbohydrates (pasta, bread, beans, and rice). Maybe you'd rather die young? Actually, the more people eat such food, the better they like it.

More and more, it looks like taking some vitamins is a good idea. Check with your doctor or someone who's knowledgeable about nutrition. *The Nutrition Action Health Letter* is a good unbiased source. See the Reading List.

Of course, you can choose not to change your habits. You can decide to eat and drink whatever you enjoy, spend most of your time sitting comfortably (or lying down), and take your chances. Just remember that it's a decision, and if you have problems, don't blame them on your age.

If you feel dragged out all the time, you may be depressed, or sick, or overworked. See your doctor and/or a therapist. Lack of energy is not normal aging.

Or maybe you're someone who's always pushed yourself as hard as you can, and your body won't let you get away with that kind of mistreatment any longer. It may be telling you to slow down. Better start to listen; you probably want this model to last a while.

Obviously, you don't have complete control over your physical condition. You can be hit by illness or disease at any age, and the odds increase as you get older. Feeling guilty won't help matters; you're not personally responsible for everything that happens to you. You do need to grieve your losses—and then move on.

And don't assume you're done for just because you're no longer in your twenties. Chronic diseases, like diabetes and arthritis, can be managed. People of all ages, injured in accidents, cope with physical disabilities every day. And even very old people can recover from illnesses.

Your general state of health, and especially your attitude, strongly affects how well you cope with whatever life deals out to you.

With physical health, as with almost everything else, that essential principle of diversity—people becoming more different from each other with age—applies. One woman may be seriously limited with arthritis in her fifties, while another climbs a ladder to paint her house at ninety-two.

Taking good care of yourself with sensible diet, exercise, and a positive attitude is more likely to land you in the ladder category.

If you really want to climb mountains at eighty-four, it would be a good idea to start preparing now. But you might want to aim for something a little less strenuous, like a local marathon.

You won't live forever; none of us will. The point of healthier habits is not so much to live longer as to live better, with fewer chronic problems and debilitating illnesses. My own goal is to die old, in relatively good health!

Chapter Nine

Galloping Ageism: Whoa!

Ten Ways to Feel Better about Not Being Younger

Galloping Ageism: Whoa!

Ten Ways to Feel Better about Not Being Younger

Ageism was defined more than thirty years ago by Dr. Robert Butler, who described it as "discrimination on the basis of age, based on myths and stereotypes about aging."

Those false ideas and rigid beliefs about aging are what we've been talking about. For a long time most people accepted them as Truth, and they caused a lot of misery for older people who believed them, and/or were treated as nonpeople because of them.

But except for a few gerontologists (people who study aging) like Butler, and some older feminists, no one paid much attention to ageism.

Until now.

With over twenty-one million people in this country between forty and forty-four, and nearly eighteen and a half million between forty-five and the Big Five-Oh, a huge chunk of the U.S. population is beginning to realize that they just don't feel like what they thought people were supposed to feel like at their age.

You don't feel washed-up, worn-out, ready to be tossed into the discard pile, do you?

One way to deal with not "feeling your age" is to decide that you're different from everyone you went to school with, and to associate only with those younger than yourself.

The problem with your solution is that, by cutting yourself off from people your own age, you don't know what they're really like. You have no one with whom to share your memories of Kennedy's assassination and the Beav. And worst of all, you still believe that getting older is a tragedy.

As long as you continue to talk and act as though aging is terrible, you'll keep yourself convinced that it is.

So here are some things you can *do* (not just read about) to change that belief (assuming you prefer not to be miserable).

1. Start by watching your language. If you use the word "young" when what you really mean is *healthy, happy, energetic, vital, creative, interesting, attractive,* and the world "old" when what you really mean is *unhealthy, miserable, sluggish, doddering, rigid, boring, ugly,* you're reinforcing your belief that remaining alive is a pretty scary proposition.

People don't really *feel* young or old; age is not a feeling. Remember how rotten you felt many times when you were young? If you believe that "feeling old" means feeling terrible, you're less likely to feel good as you grow older.

I feel a hundred years old.

If you find yourself saying, "I feel the same inside as I did twenty years ago," or "I'm forty-five but I feel twenty-five," stop and think of what you were like back then. You've changed a lot inside as well as outside. What you probably mean is that you're still a vital human being—and that makes sense, because vitality, energy, and enthusiasm are not age-limited.

Hey,
dude ₒₒₒ

I'm 52
funky years
old

Become aware of how often
the old are called names—old
biddy, old bag, geezer—and
avoid those words. Terms that put people down because of their
racial or ethnic groups, their disabilities, or their sexual or affectional
preference are not generally acceptable in print or in polite society.
Why should they be for the old?

If such words continue to be tossed around,
you'll find yourself the
target sooner than you
might think.

Am I
old yet?

2. If someone says you don't look your age, try not to smile and say "Thank you." If you do, you're accepting the Myth of Loss of Looks. (Women are likely to have an especially hard time with this one, because the moment they emerged from the womb, the Wicked Oh-Lay Fairy whispered to them, "Beautiful means young"; a true curse.)

You can say: "If you mean you find me attractive, thank you!"

You can always give the famous Steinem response: "This is what forty [or whatever] looks like."

If you're feeling a little belligerent, you can ask, "What am I *supposed* to look like at my age?"

Or you can simply ignore the remark.

3. If you buy hostile birthday cards that ridicule age, give some thought to what you're doing. Bashing your friend, relative, colleague, partner, or spouse is, in effect, also bashing yourself, or your future self. It's unlikely to help you—or them—look forward to the next birthday.

It's interesting that disabilities such as blindness, difficulty walking, and memory loss are not generally considered a laughing matter except when they're associated with age.

4. If you make hostile jokes about your own aging, such as saying, "I must be getting Alzheimer's disease" when you forget something, *stop!*

As you know from learning about the Myth of Memory Loss, Alzheimer's is a disease that afflicts a minority of elders, and it's not funny. Would you say, "I must be getting cancer" or "I must be getting lupus" and expect a laughing response?

With someone your own age, of course, you can gain comfort from sharing your genuine predicaments, such as finding that you have to move print farther and farther away to be able to read it. (My standard joke used to be that my arms were getting shorter!)

But if all your remarks refer to the Three D's (disease, disability, and death), you're going to be pretty miserable after a while. And other people are going to believe that you're falling apart, mentally and physically. Is that really what you want? In today's job market, it could be dangerous.

5. If you're invited to a black balloon party, bring a red one that says something like "Welcome to the Fabulous Fifies." The craze for funereal birthday parties fortunately seems to be passing and perhaps soon will be buried six feet under, where it belongs. There's something pretty crazy in the notion that remaining alive is the worst thing that could possibly happen to you.

6. Learn to identify ageism in advertising, and write to complain about it. (You can spread the complaint more widely by posting it on the Net!) Threaten to stop buying the product, even if it's something you never use.

7. Voice your objections to magazine and newspaper articles and movies that portray growing older only as a problem and the old as incompetents, oddballs, or pathetic whining creatures. Cancel subscriptions; write letters to the editor. Short snappy ones are more likely to be effective—and to be published.

8. If you have the power to change the way aging is portrayed by the media in a major way—as an editor, writer, filmmaker, advertiser, or anyone who works in media industries—do so. You'll be on the cutting edge.

As a media watcher for the past ten years, I can assure you that, even though it may not look that way to you, age-positive messages have increased by leaps and bounds over the past couple of years. And there's no reason to believe that the trend won't continue. There are lots and lots of people around just waiting to get old.

I am.
therefore
I am.

9. If you've been lying about your age because you hate growing older, you might consider accepting yourself for who you are. Trying to "pass" as younger is stressful, though it does provide good exercise for your memory, since you constantly have to remember *not* to remember any of the events that would give your age away!

Of course, you may hide your age because you're afraid you'll lose a job, or that people will treat you differently if they know how old you are. With all the ageism around, your fears aren't groundless.

But you'll be better equipped to deal with age discrimination if you know the facts about aging, and if you feel positive about growing older.

Increasingly, age discrimination suits are successful—perhaps in part because many of those who decide them are older themselves.

10. Throw a big party for your next birthday, and let people know that, because you're looking forward to the rest of your life, you don't want negative cards. Life-affirming greetings are slowly creeping into the market. They aren't all serious or sentimental; ridiculing age is only one form of humor.

You'll be giving your guests a gift, and you'll feel good reading the cards they come up with.

If you have children, a change in your attitude is a gift you can give to them as well. Your feelings about aging are probably a lot like those of your parents. If they feel (or felt) that growing older is a tragedy, you're more likely to think so too.

Challenging galloping ageism can make you a winner, feeling better about yourself and more willing to move on with your life

Chapter Ten

Far Better than the Alternative

The Advantages of Aging

We have
a lot in
common.

Far Better than the Alternative

The Advantages of Aging

You may have become so accustomed to hearing people moan and groan about growing older that you've never stopped to consider what's *good* about it— beyond the obvious answer that it's better than being dead.

So stop and ask yourself: what have you gained from living?

For one thing, you're almost certainly more self-confident than you used to be Remember how you used to worry about what people thought of you, about making mistakes, about whether you could make it in the grown-up world?

Well, here you are, and you're doing OK.

You don't worry so much about what other people think of you because you know yourself better than you used to, and have more confidence in your own judgment.

Talk to me.

You've found that *not* listening to your own inner voice, your "gut feeling," gets you into trouble. So you're more likely to pay attention to what it's saying.

And not worrying so much about other people's opinions gives you the freedom to take risks, to make mistakes. Living as long as you have, you've probably tripped over yourself a number of times—and you know that it's not the end of the world. In fact, making mistakes is probably one of the most effective (if painful) ways to learn.

Anything that didn't kill me, made me stronger.

One reason you don't worry so much about what other people think of you is that you've realized most of them *don't* think of you, most of the time. In other words, you've discovered that you're not the center of the universe—a humbling but very freeing realization.

Unless you're a public figure and the media picks up on it, you can make a fool of yourself in public, and most people (with the probable exception of a spouse or partner!) will have forgotten what you did by the end of the day, if not by the end of the hour or minute.

If you tend to be a perfectionist, you've probably become more accepting of your failures and foibles, having lived with yourself longer. You've found that people like you even though you're not perfect—in fact, people like you *more* when they realize you're not perfect. You may still work to change things you don't like about yourself, but you don't beat yourself up the way you used to.

If you've spent most of your life trying to please everyone by being a doormat, you've realized by now that doormats get walked on. And that you can't please everyone, no matter what you do. So you've become more assertive.

To your surprise, you've found that you can tolerate other people's irritation and anger, and you feel better about yourself than you did when they were wiping their feet on you.

Another advantage of growing older
is that you've survived quite a few
crises, and when things go wrong,
you're less likely to panic. Difficult
situations get worked out, one way or
another—maybe not as you would have
wished, but life goes on.

With more living under your belt,
you've begun to develop a sense of perspective. Sometimes, looking
back, you even become aware that events which seemed totally
negative at the time produced some positive results later on.

Well whadya
know...

You've also accepted the fact that life isn't fair. You're less likely to waste time and energy being angry about it, and more likely to figure out what, if anything, you can do about it.

As time goes on, you're more willing to accept responsibility for yourself, and less eager to blame all your problems on others, especially your parents. You may have begun to see them as ordinary imperfect human beings with lives of their own, rather than as people who exist primarily in relation to yourself. (Becoming a parent can have this effect.) And so you're on your way to an adult relationship with them, which is likely to improve all your relationships.

Particularly if you're male, you may find yourself becoming less competitive. Winning doesn't seem nearly as important as it used to. Since you're more comfortable with yourself, you don't have so much to prove.

When you stop to look at yourself, you find that you have become a richer, fuller, more interesting person. Everything you've been through, everyone you've met, everything you've learned, has added new dimensions to your personality. You know a lot more, you understand a lot more, you're a more complete human being.

And having accepted the reality that life does not go on forever, you value it more. You may find yourself becoming more spiritual, though not necessarily more religious.

If you're saying, "But I'm not there yet!" that's OK, as long as you're heading in that direction. In any case, you never will be "all grown up," with all your problems and difficulties sorted out. You'll keep growing and changing as long as you're willing to put some effort into it.

If *none* of these advantages of aging ring true for you, you might want to stop and take a close look at yourself. Ask yourself where you're heading, and if you really want to go farther in that direction.

It most people dislike you, it's certainly time to take a look at what you're doing. If you're rigid and miserable in your forties and fifties, you're unlikely to become lovable in your seventies and eighties.

Bah everything

(Scrooge did it, but he went through some pretty traumatic experiences to get there!)

You may have got stuck—in anger or depression—and need something or someone to get you moving again. (See "A Therapist's Afterword.")

If you feel good about your age, you'll probably find even more good things to say about it. To borrow a cliché, Nothing succeeds like success. So enjoy!

109

Chapter Eleven

If You're Backing into Middle Age, You Don't Know Where You're Going

How to Turn Yourself Around and Look Forward to Living

If You're Backing into Middle Age, You Don't Know Where You're Going

How to Turn Yourself Around and Look Forward to Living

Except as a party game, walking backward, or even walking forward with your eyes tightly shut, doesn't make a lot of sense unless you like bumping into things. But that's the way a lot of people approach aging.

Would you move to a new city or country without learning anything about it, without preparing for the move?

By reading this book, you've turned yourself around, opened your eyes, and learned something about the territory you're entering. You've found it's a far better place than you thought it was, and that there's a lot you can do to make it even better—physically, psychologically, and practically.

To summarize:

Physically, it's a good idea to:

- Get regular exercise.

- Treat your body with respect.

- Eat a reasonably healthy diet.

- Use alcohol moderately or not at all.

- Not smoke or use drugs.

Mentally, it's a good idea to:

- Challenge ageism.

  - Love and accept yourself as you are now.

    - Accept and adapt to change; be flexible.

    - Learn something new on a regular basis.

- Ask for help if you're feeling overwhelmed.

- Have friends of all ages. You can learn and benefit from both younger and older friends, and they from you.

- Maintain a wide range of interests, so you won't be totally lost if one activity goes down the tubes.

Practically, it's a good idea to:

- Do some financial planning. It's never too soon, or too late, to start, though the sooner the better. You need a balance between salting so much away that you can't enjoy living, and spending so much that you put nothing away and are awash in debt.

- Assume responsibility for your own health care. With all the changes taking place in the health care system, it's important to be assertive about getting the care you need. Learn about your body,

keep track of your medical treatment, ask your doctors questions, insist on answers. Don't let anyone write off real problems to "age."

- Prepare an "advance directive"—such as a Living Will and/or a Durable Power of Attorney for Health Care—which states what you'd want done (or not done) if you should become unable to make such decisions yourself. It makes sense to have such an instrument at any age.

You'll never have complete control over what life deals out to you. But you do have control over what you do with it.

However you live your life, the main thing is to experience it fully, and not let fears of growing older keep you from having a good time.

So let's get on with it!!

The end.

Well, only if you're a pessimist.

Chapter Twelve

A Therapist's Afterword

Anything that didn't kill me, made me stronger.

A Therapist's Afterword

As a psychologist and therapist who has a specialty in geriatrics but works with clients of all ages, I have a few thoughts in a more serious vein.

Several times in this book, I refer to depression and anxiety, which are associated not only with fears of aging, but also with other stresses common at midlife. Both are miserable, and treatable; there's no need to suffer in silence

Some people are helped by therapy or counseling, others by medication. The most effective treatment is often a combination of the two.

If you're addicted to alcohol or drugs, do something about it. Your life will be a mess until you do, because the addictions keep you from learning better ways to deal with problems. Obviously, your life won't magically straighten around if you quit, but it's a start. Some people go to treatment, others use twelve-step or other recovery groups. You can try to stop on your own, but that's a lot harder and may leave you with many of the problems that led to the addiction in the first place. Again, working with a good therapist can help you develop new means of coping with the stresses of your life.

If issues of your own (or your parents') aging, and especially fears of aging, are a major part of your concern, it's a good idea to look for someone with specialized training, who knows about normal aging and about normal changes that can affect treatment. (For example, dosages of most medications should be smaller as people age, since the liver metabolizes them less efficiently.) Geriatrics, the treatment of older adults, is a growing specialty, as is gerontology, the study of aging—including midlife. The number of such specialists is still limited; call your local referral services for recommendations.

It's helpful to work with a person who is not only knowledgeable about aging, but who has come to terms with his or her own aging and mortality. That doesn't necessarily mean someone older than yourself. Some physicians and therapists have been fortunate enough to grow up in families where parents didn't complain about growing older or allow age to limit their lives unnecessarily. And some have had a life-threatening experience at an earlier age—which usually cures people of the fear of aging; they're glad simply to be alive.

If you have a parent with a serious or terminal illness, you're probably grieving and, if you're a caregiver, stressed out. You may also find yourself worrying more about your own aging. Just remember that you are not your parents. You are yourself, with a different life history from theirs. Your parents probably did not plan to live as long as they have; you can plan for your old age, physically, mentally, and financially. Starting early gives you a real edge.

If your parent has a disease or illness that runs in the family, learn what you can about causes and prevention, and start taking action. For example, my mother may have had Alzheimer's disease, and the jury is still out on the role of aluminum in that disease. So I hedge my bets by cooking with stainless steel and using nonaluminum deodorants.

Growing old is not easy—but then, life is not always easy for children, adolescents, young adults, or the middle-aged either. The trick is to accommodate, adjust, trim your sails to the wind. It's a lifelong process. Sometimes the water is smooth, and sometimes it's stormy. But the company is great, and the scenery can be spectacular!

A Reading List

For People Who Want to Know a Little More —or a Lot

A Reading List

For People Who Want to Know a Little More—or a Lot

The following reading list is certainly not comprehensive, but suggests several resources for anyone who wants to read more about aging. If you would like to share the names of your favorite books or newsletters, just send a note to: "Old Is Not a Four-Letter Word," c/o Papier-Mache Press, 627 Walker Street, Watsonville, CA 95076.

Books

William H. Bergquist, with Elinor M. Greenberg and S. Alan Klaum. *In Our Fifties: Voices of Men and Women Reinventing Their Lives.* Jossey-Bass, 1993. Terrified of turning fifty? This book, based on personal interviews with more than seventy women and men, may give you some more positive ideas.

Lydia Bronte. *The Longevity Factor.* Harper Perennial, 1993. If you're wondering what to do with the rest of your life, take a look at this book, based on interviews with 150 people between the ages of 65 and 101 who at the time were still actively involved in jobs or careers.

Robert Butler, MD, and Myrna Lewis. *Love and Sex after Sixty.* Revised Edition. Ballantine Books, 1993. Even if you're not sixty yet, you might want to check this out if you're having sexual problems, or if you have a spouse or lover who is older—male or female.

Margaret Cruikshank, ed. *Fierce with Reality: An Anthology of Literature on Aging.* North Star Press, 1995. A collection of poems, short stories, folktales, interviews, and essays mirroring the richness of aging around the world, for dipping into.

Paula Brown Doress and Diana Laskin Siegal. *Ourselves, Growing Older: Women Aging with Knowledge and Power.* Simon & Schuster, 1987; revised edition 1994. The grown-up version of *Our Bodies, Our Selves.* Full of useful and interesting information about all aspects of women's aging.

Mark Edinberg. *Talking with Your Aging Parents.* Shambhala, 1988. An excellent guide if you're concerned about Mom and Dad. Notice that its "talking *with*," not "talking *to.*"

Betty Friedan. *The Fountain of Age.* Simon & Schuster, 1993. Heavy going, but full of positive information and positive ideas about aging. If you think you're too young for this one, it could be a good gift for a lively minded parent or grand parent, who could then tell you all about it!

Mark Gerzon. *Listening to Midlife: Turning Your Crisis into a Quest.* Shambhala, 1996. Especially if you're a man and you're feeling gloomy about turning fifty, you'll be informed and inspired by this account of a boomer's midlife and what he's learned along the way.

Connie Goldman and Richard Mahler. *Secrets of Becoming a Late Bloomer: Extraordinary Ordinary People on the Art of Staying Creative, Alive, and Aware in Mid-Life and Beyond*. Still Point Publishing, 1995. If you listen to National Public Radio, you may have heard Goldman, who has been talking positively about aging on radio and elsewhere for over fifteen years.

Sadja Greenwood, MD. *Menopause, Naturally: Preparing for the Second Half of Life*. Volcano Press, 1984; revised edition 1992. This book emphasizes the normality of menopause and suggests natural means for accommodating its manifestations. One of the earliest and best books on the subject.

David Gutmann, PhD. *Reclaimed Powers: Toward a New Psychology of Men and Women in Later Life*. Basic Books, 1987. For anyone who wants to know a lot more about the Midlife Crossover, in this country and in various cultures.

The Hen Co-op. *Growing Old Disgracefully* and *Disgracefully Yours*. Crossing Press, 1994 and 1996. For a highly personal, useful, funny, and interesting read, pick up these cooperative works by six women; "ideas for getting the most out of life."

Ruth Harriet Jacobs. *Be an Outrageous Older Woman, a RASP—Remarkable Aging Smart Person*. KIT, 1991. A natural teacher full of energy, creativity, and good humor, Jacobs will guide you into being that more assertive self after your Midlife Crossover. She's another long-time activist.

Danielle C. Lapp. *Don't Forget! Easy Exercises for a Better Memory at Any Age*. McGraw-Hill, 1987; revised edition, Addison-Wesley, 1995. I like this book because it's knowledgeable about aging, has lots of diagrams, and includes good exercises (few of which, I must admit, I have ever done myself!).

Sandra Haldeman Martz, ed. *When I Am an Old Woman I Shall Wear Purple*. Papier-Mache Press, 1987. If you haven't seen this bestselling anthology of poetry, fiction, and photographs, where have you been? Like *Old Is Not a Four-Letter Word*, it views aging as a gift of nature.

Sandra Haldeman Martz, ed. *Grow Old Along with Me—The Best Is Yet to Be.* Papier-Mache Press, 1996. A fine companion volume to When I Am an Old Woman.

Cathleen Rountree. *Coming into Our Fullness: On Women Turning Forty.* Crossing Press, 1991. If you have concerns about turning forty, or being in that decade, this collection of photographs and interviews with eighteen women between forty and fifty should change your perspective.

Cathleen Rountree. *On Women Turning 50: Celebrating Mid-Life Discoveries.* HarperSanFrancisco, 1993. Same as above, only for fifty—personal stories of survival and success, by eighteen women.

Jim Smoke. *Facing 50: A View from the Mountaintop. How to Enjoy the Most Rewarding Years of Your Life.* Thomas Nelson, 1994. Obviously, a book with an attitude—a positive one.

Dena Taylor and Amber Coverdale Sumrall, eds. *Women of the 14th Moon: Writings on Menopause.* Crossing Press, 1991. A very diverse collection of prose and poetry by ninety women; whatever your menopause experience, you'll find it here!

Dena Taylor and Amber Coverdale Sumrall, eds. *The Time of Our Lives: Women Write on Sex after 40.* Crossing Press, 1993. Sixty-six stories by women from their forties to their eighties. Everything you ever wanted to know but were afraid to ask!

Helen Rippier Wheeler. *Women and Aging: A Guide to the Literature.* Lynne Reinner Publishers, 1997. If you really want to know more about any aspect of women's aging, here are 2,000 resources you can check out!

Newsletters

These can be a good way of keeping up with current information about health, nutrition, and wellness. Most are monthly publications with a relatively low annual fee.

Consumer Reports on Health. Like the magazine, published by the nonprofit Consumers Union. Box 56356, Boulder, CO 80322-6356.

Harvard Men's Health Watch. P.O. Box 420097, Palm Coast, FL 32142-8895. "Information for enlightened choices from Harvard Medical School."

Harvard Women's Health Watch. P.O. Box 420234, Palm Coast, FL 32142-0234. Ditto from Harvard Medical School.

Johns Hopkins Medical Letter: Health after 50. P.O. Box 420179, Palm Coast, FL 32142. "Taking control of your own health and medical care."

Nutrition Action Health Newsletter. Published by the Center for Science in the Public Interest. 1875 Connecticut Avenue, NW, Suite 300, Washington, DC 20009-5728. Good unbiased information on food and nutrition. Don't read this if you want to continue to eat a lot of junk food.

University of California at Berkeley Wellness Letter. Published by the School of Public Health at UC Berkeley. P.O. Box 420148, Palm Coast, FL 32142. "The newsletter of nutrition, fitness, and stress management."

Women's Health Advocate Newsletter. P.O. Box 420235, Palm Coast, FL 32142. "An independent voice on women's wellness."

Obviously, those people down in Palm Coast keep busy sending out newsletters! Do you suppose they're using senior power?

More Papier-Mache Press Titles of Related Interest

When I Am an Old Woman I Shall Wear Purple
Edited by Sandra Haldeman Martz

Winner of a 1991 American Booksellers Book of the Year Honors Award, *When I Am an Old Woman I Shall Wear Purple* takes a refreshing look at the issues of aging in a society that glorifies youth. This remarkable collection evokes the beauty, humor, and courage of women living in their later years and tells of the endearing moments of joy and passion to be found in the rich and varied world of midlife and beyond. These simple, compelling words share the universal message of aging as a natural gift of life.

"Tending toward the emotive and always from the subjective, these pieces articulate what it is like to be Everywoman from every age." —Library Journal

ISBN 0-918949-16-5, trade paper, ISBN 0-918949-15-7, hardcover
ISBN 0-918949-83-1, large print

Kitchen Tables (and Other Midlife Musings)
Niela Eliason

Niela Eliason captures the lively essence of daily life and its accompanying memories for anyone in their midlife years. These essays are a treasure chest of the insightful thoughts, feelings, and opinions of our middle-aged generation—trusting chicken soup, staying married, and sharing stories around the kitchen table.

"Have a seat at Niela Eliason's kitchen table. You'll enjoy the stories she's going to tell you." —Tony Hillerman

ISBN 0-918949-62-9, trade paper

About the Author

Ann Gerike has been reading, writing, and speaking about aging and ageism for fifteen years. After a midlife career change, she moved to Houston and completed her PhD in clinical psychology with a fellowship in gerontology in 1983. Six years later she moved to Minneapolis—"out of the frying pan into the freezer." A licensed psychologist, she currently has a private practice as a psychotherapist in Minneapolis and provides workshops on aging and ageism. She is the mother of David, Peggy, and Cathy, the mother-in-law of Sam, and the grandmother of Jeremiah Daniel.

Listed in *Who's Who in America* and *Who's Who of American Women* since 1992, she is a member of the American Psychological Association, the American Society on Aging, the Minnesota Psychological Association, the Minnesota Gerontological Society, Minnesota Women Psychologists (and Steering Committee member since 1995), National Women's Studies Association (and convenor of the Aging and Ageism Caucus, 1986–1995), and a board member of the Twin Cities Gray Panthers.

About the Illustrator

Peter Kohlsaat—longtime syndicated cartoonist, illustrator, fisherman, and former dentist—is hard at work attempting to create the perfect job: getting paid to have adventures. Along with his dog, Zelda—watchdog, copilot, cow spotter, and former humane society resident, who already has the perfect job—they can be found driving America's back roads in search of fishing hot spots or on a beach somewhere chasing the good life.

Papier-Mache Press

At Papier-Mache Press, it is our goal to identify and successfully present important social issues through enduring works of beauty, grace, and strength. Through our work we hope to encourage empathy and respect among diverse communities, creating a bridge of understanding between the mainstream audience and those who might not otherwise be heard.

We appreciate you, our customer, and strive to earn your continued support. We also value the role of the bookseller in achieving our goals. We are especially grateful to the many independent booksellers whose presence ensure a continuing diversity of opinion, information, and literature in our communities. We encourage you to support these bookstores with your patronage.

We publish many fine books about women's experiences. We also produce lovely posters and T-shirts that complement our anthologies. Please ask your local bookstore which Papier-Mache items they carry. To receive our complete catalog, send your request to Papier-Mache Press, 627 Walker Street, Watsonville, CA 95076, or call our toll-free number, 800-927-5913.